El Salvador

by Joyce Markovics

Consultant: Marjorie Faulstich Orellana, PhD
Professor of Urban Schooling
University of California, Los Angeles

New York, New York

Credits

Cover, © CREATISTA/Shutterstock and © Milosz_M/Shutterstock; TOC, © rook76/Shutterstock; 4, © GomezDavid/Shutterstock; 5L, © Vladimir Melnik/Shutterstock; 5R, © digi_guru/iStock; 7, © Ekrystia/Dreamstime; 8–9, © edfuentesg/iStock; 10, © jose Luis Ocejo/Thinkstock; 11, © bikerlondon/Shutterstock; 12, © Ddanita Delimont Creative/Alamy; 13, © worldswildlifewonders/Shutterstock; 13T, © Martin Fowler/Shutterstock; 14, © GomezDavid/iStock; 14B, © PisitBurana/iStock; 15, © GomezDavid/iStock; 16–17, © Raymona Pooler/Shutterstock; 18, © dbimages/Alamy; 19, © Andre Nantel/Shutterstock; 20, © Vespasian/Alamy; 21, © Thornton Cohen/Alamy; 22, © Quang Ho/Shutterstock; 23, © Jan Sochor; 24, © Photographerlondon/Dreamstime; 25L, © Roberto A Sanchez/iStock; 25R, © Sarah Bossert/iStock; 26, © vm2002/Shutterstock; 27, © Julie Feinstein/Dreamstime; 28, © Jamie Robinson/Shutterstock; 29T, © donatas1205/Shutterstock; 29B, © Stefano Ember/Shutterstock; 30T, © fourleaflover/Shutterstock; 30M, © nimon/Shutterstock; 30B, © bilgehan yilmaz/iStock; 31 (T to B), © Andre Nantel/Shutterstock, © bikerlondon/Shutterstock, © Milosz_M/Shutterstock, © moxelotle/iStock, and © Ekrystia/Dreamstime.

Publisher: Kenn Goin
Senior Editor: Joyce Tavolacci
Creative Director: Spencer Brinker
Design: Debrah Kaiser

Library of Congress Cataloging-in-Publication Data

Markovics, Joyce L.
  El Salvador / by Joyce Markovics.
     pages cm. — (Countries we come from)
  Includes bibliographical references and index.
  Audience: Ages 5–8.
  ISBN 978-1-62724-859-4 (library binding) — ISBN 1-62724-859-5 (library binding)
  1. El Salvador—Juvenile literature. I. Title.
  F1483.2.M37 2015
  972.84—dc23
                                         2015004784

For more information, write to Bearport Publishing Company, Inc., 45 West 21st Street, Suite 3B, New York, New York 10010. Printed in the United States of America.

10 9 8 7 6 5 4 3 2 1

Contents

CORREOS AEREO

TALAPO

EUMOMOTA SUPERCILIOSA APIASTER

20ᶜ EL SALVADOR. C.A.

This Is El Salvador

HILLY

Colorful

Full of history

El Salvador is the smallest country in Central America.

Yet it has a large **population** for its size.

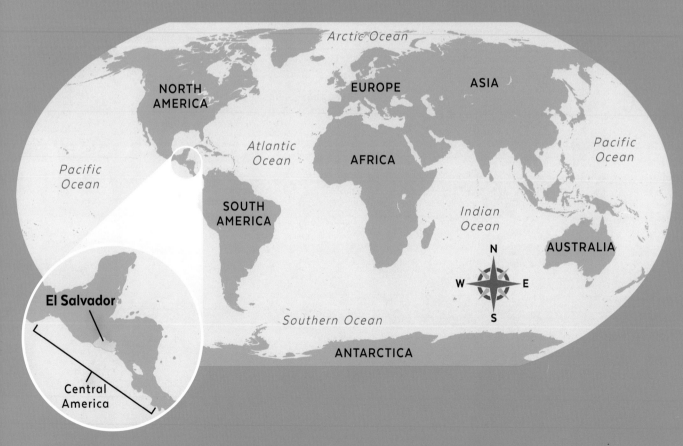

More than six million people live in El Salvador.

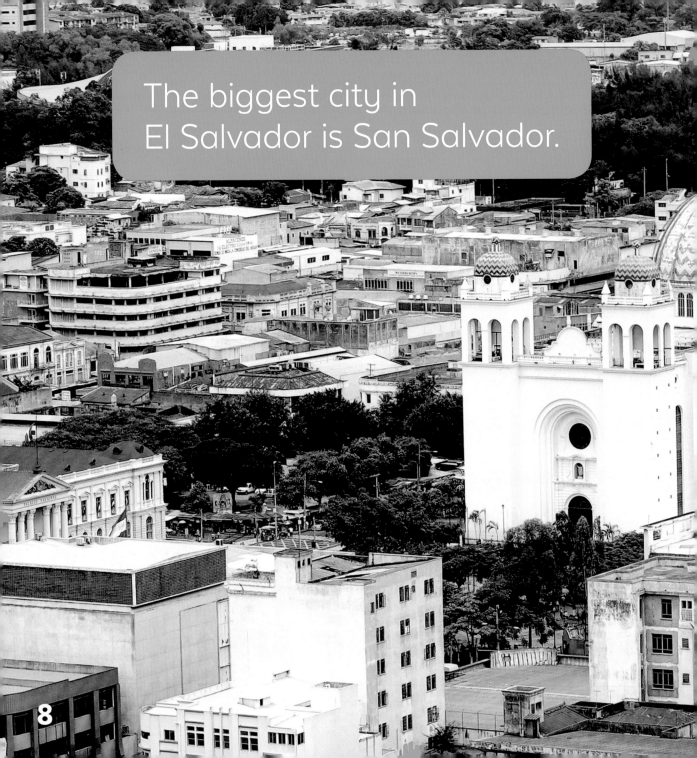

The biggest city in
El Salvador is San Salvador.

It's also the country's **capital**. Many people live and work there.

San Salvador was founded in 1525.

The country has **plains**, forests, and mountains.

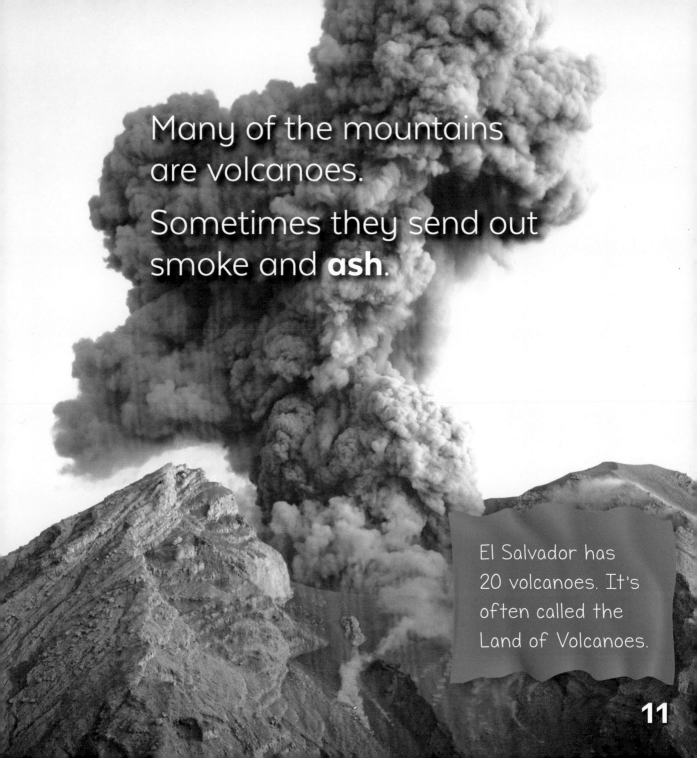

Many of the mountains are volcanoes.

Sometimes they send out smoke and **ash**.

El Salvador has 20 volcanoes. It's often called the Land of Volcanoes.

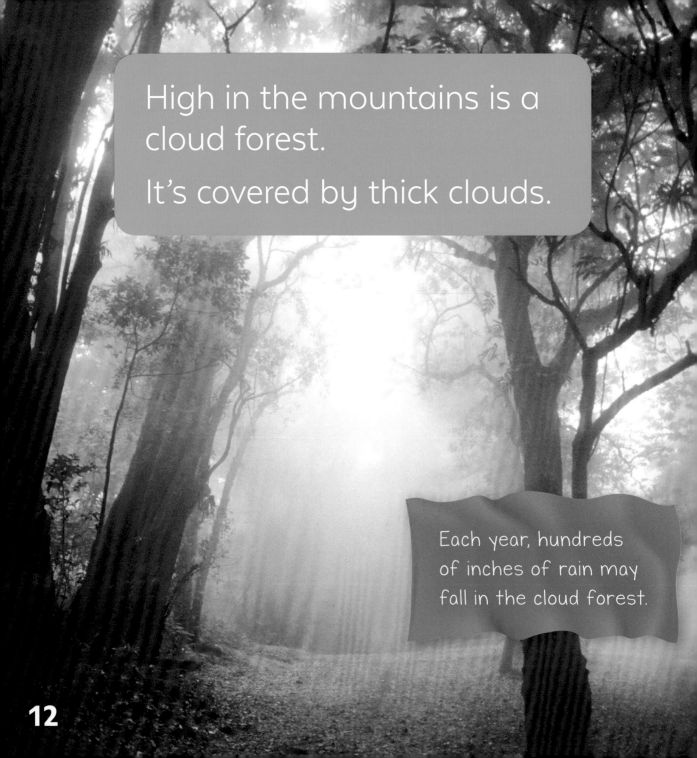

High in the mountains is a cloud forest.

It's covered by thick clouds.

Each year, hundreds of inches of rain may fall in the cloud forest.

Plants such as orchids grow on trees in the forest.

orchid flowers

Birds, monkeys, and jaguars also live there.

13

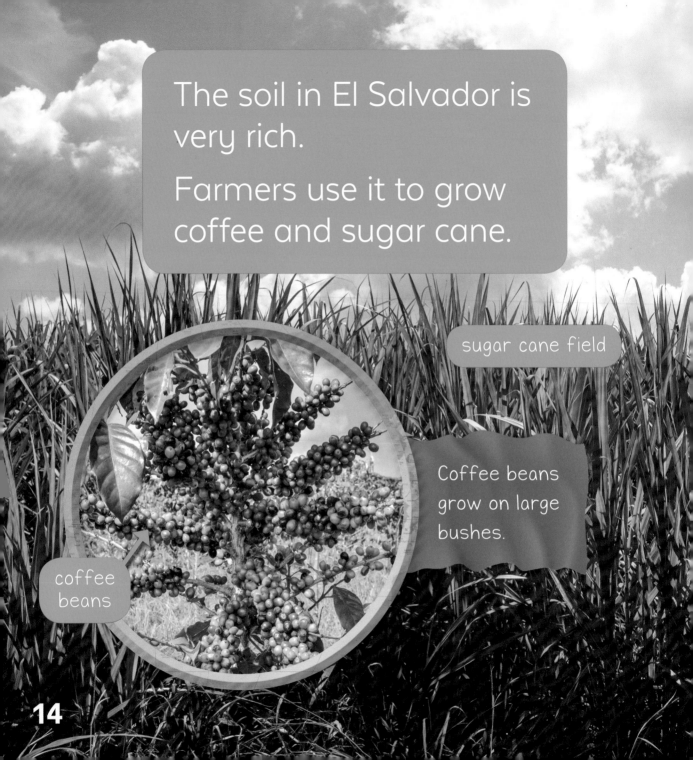

The soil in El Salvador is very rich.

Farmers use it to grow coffee and sugar cane.

sugar cane field

Coffee beans grow on large bushes.

coffee beans

They also raise cows on the grassy plains.

El Salvador has a long history.
Indians called the Olmecs settled there about 4,000 years ago.

Later, other groups arrived, including the Maya and Pipil Indians.

Maya pyramid at Tazumal

The Maya built huge stone pyramids.

The Spanish arrived in the 1500s.

Today, most Salvadorans are mestizos.

mestizo man

They are part Spanish and part Indian.

The Spanish word *mestizos* means "mixed."

Pipil woman

Many Salvadorans are **descendants** of the Pipil Indians.

19

Most Salvadorans speak Spanish.
This is how you say *hello* in
Spanish:

Hola (OH-lah)

This is how you say *good-bye*:

Salu (sa-LOO)

or

Adiós (ah-dee-YOHS)

More than 450 million people around the world speak Spanish.

El Salvador has lots of colorful festivals.

In May, there is a festival of flowers.

People parade through the streets.

They carry huge bunches of flowers.

The flower festival dates back to Mayan times.

When some Salvadoran girls turn 15, they have a big party.

It's called a Quinceañera (KEEN-se-an-YEH-rah).

Everyone dresses up.

The birthday girl gets lots of presents—and a big cake.

Girls pick out colorful gowns for their party.

What do people eat in El Salvador?

The main foods are rice, beans, and pupusas.

rice and beans

Pupusas are thick tortillas (tor-TEE-*yahs*) stuffed with tasty fillings.

pupusa

Tortillas are flat corn or wheat pancakes.

Salvadorans love to play soccer.

It's the most popular sport in the country.

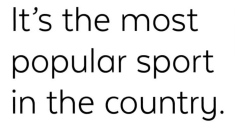

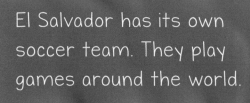

El Salvador has its own soccer team. They play games around the world.

People play on fields, streets, and even on beaches!

Fast Facts

Capital city:
San Salvador

Population of El Salvador:
More than six million

Main language:
Spanish

Money: U.S. dollar

Major religions: Roman Catholic and
Protestant Christian

Neighboring countries:
Honduras and Guatemala

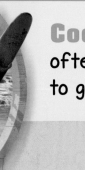

Cool Fact: People
often visit El Salvador
to go surfing.

ash (ASH) tiny volcanic pieces of rock and minerals

capital (KAP-uh-tuhl) a city where a country's government is based

descendants (di-SEND-uhnts) people that come from a family that lived at an earlier time

plains (PLAYNZ) large, flat areas of land

population (pop-yuh-LAY-shuhn) the total number of people living in a place

Glossary

31

Index

Read More

Foley, Erin. *El Salvador (Cultures of the World).* New York: Cavendish Square Publishing (2005).

Simmons, Walter. *El Salvador (Exploring Countries).* Minneapolis, MN: Bellwether Media (2012).

Learn More Online

To learn more about El Salvador, visit
www.bearportpublishing.com/CountriesWeComeFrom

About the Author

Joyce Markovics lives far from El Salvador in Tarrytown, New York.